Augustus Welby Northmore Pugin

An Apology for the Revival of Christian Architecture in England

Augustus Welby Northmore Pugin

An Apology for the Revival of Christian Architecture in England

ISBN/EAN: 9783337026868

Printed in Europe, USA, Canada, Australia, Japan

Cover: Foto ©Lupo / pixelio.de

More available books at **www.hansebooks.com**

AN APOLOGY

FOR

The Revival of Christian Architecture

IN

ENGLAND.

BY

A. WELBY PUGIN,

ARCHITECT,

LATE PROFESSOR OF ECCLESIASTICAL ANTIQUITIES AT ST. MARIE'S COLLEGE, OSCOTT.

Edinburgh
JOHN GRANT
31 GEORGE IV. BRIDGE
1895

✠ To the Right Honourable

The Earl of Shrewsbury, Waterford, and Wexford.

My very good Lord,

It would be most unnatural and ungrateful in me, when putting forth a Treatise relating to the Revival of Christian Architecture in England, were I not to dedicate the same in an especial manner to your Lordship, who has been the main support in the furtherance of that good work, and to whom I am so greatly bounden.

May God in his mercy grant, that as your Lordship's noble ancestor, the Talbot of famous memory, extended the temporal glory of England by deeds of arms, so may your Lordship continue to increase the spiritual welfare of these realms by reviving the ancient glories of the English Church, of whose faith your noble house has furnished so many witnesses.

That your Lordship may long be blessed with health and strength to carry out to a happy conclusion the many good designs you have in hand, is the constant prayer of

Your Lordship's devoted and faithful Bedesman,

✠ A. Welby Pugin.

LIST OF PLATES.

PLATE I. FRONTISPIECE.

  II. Buildings of the time of Francis I. . . . *to face p.* 8

  III. Railways 10

  IV. Cemetery Company's Entrance 12

  V.   Revived Sepulchral Brasses 34

  VI. Do. 36

  VII. Domestic Buildings 39

  VIII. Examples of Christian Sculpture 43

  IX. Paintings of the Christian and revived Pagan artists compared 44

  X.   Church Furniture revived at Birmingham . . . 51

REFERENCES TO THE FRONTISPIECE.

1. St. George's, London.
2. St. Peter's, Woolwich.
3. St. Marie's, Stockton.
4. St. Giles's, Cheadle.
5. St. Marie's, Newcastle-on-Tyne.
6. North Gate, St. Marie's, Oscott.
7. St. Austin's, Kenilworth.
8. Jesus Chapel, Pomfret.
9. Cathedral, Killarney.
10. St. Chad's, Birmingham.
11. St. Oswald's, Liverpool.
12. Holy Cross, Kirkham.
13. St. Barnabas, Nottingham.
14. Gorey, Ireland.
15. St. Marie's, Derby.
16. St. Alban's, Macclesfield.
17. St. Marie's, Brewood.
18. St. Winifride's, Shepshead.
19. St. Andrew's, Cambridge.
20. St. Bernard's Priory, Leicestershire.
21. St. Marie's, Keighley.
22. St. Marie's, Warwick Bridge.
23. St. Wilfrid's, Manchester.
24. St. Marie's, Southport.
25. St. John's Hospital, Alton.

AN APOLOGY

FOR

THE REVIVAL OF CHRISTIAN ARCHITECTURE IN ENGLAND.

HE age in which we live is a most eventful period for English art. We are just emerging from a state which may be termed the dark ages of architecture. After a gradual decay of four centuries, the style,—for style there was,—became so execrably bad, that the cup of degradation was filled to the brim; and as taste had fallen to its lowest depth, a favourable re-action commenced.

The breaking up of this wretched state of things has naturally produced a complete convulsion in the whole system of arts, and a Babel of confusion has succeeded to the one bad idea that generally prevailed.

Private judgment runs riot; every architect has a theory of his own, a beau ideal he has himself created; a disguise with which to invest the building he erects. This is generally the result of his latest travels. One breathes nothing but the Alhambra,—another the Parthenon,—a third is full of lotus cups and pyramids from the banks of the Nile,—a fourth, from Rome, is all dome and basilica; whilst another works Stuart and Revett on a modified plan, and builds lodges, centenary chapels, reading-rooms, and fish markets, with small Doric work and white brick facings. Styles are now *adopted* instead of *generated*, and ornament and design *adapted to*, instead of *originated by*, the edifices themselves.

This may, indeed, be appropriately termed the *carnival* of architecture: its professors appear tricked out in the guises of all centuries and all nations; the Turk and the Christian, the Egyptian and the Greek, the Swiss and the Hindoo, march side by side, and mingle together; and some of these gentlemen, not satisfied with perpetrating one character, appear in two or three costumes in the same evening.[1]

Amid this motley group (oh! miserable degradation!) the venerable form and sacred detail of our national and Catholic architecture may be discerned; but *how* adopted? Not on consistent principle, not on authority, not as the expression of our faith, our government, or country, but as one of the disguises of the day, to be put on and off at pleasure, and used occasionally as circumstances or private caprice may suggest.

It is considered suitable for some purposes,—MELANCHOLY, and *therefore fit for religious* buildings!!! a style that an architect of the day should be acquainted with, in order to please those who admire old things,[2]—a style in which there are many beauties: such is the heartless advocacy which our national architecture frequently receives from its professed admirers; while others are not wanting, even in the most influential positions, who venture to sneer at and insult its principles, either because they are far beyond their comprehension, or that they

---

[1] It is not unusual for architects to send two designs for the same building, of utterly opposed character and style, for the selection of the committee; as if it were possible for more than one principle to be a correct expression of the intended building.

[2] If a pointed design is sent, it is generally in accordance with the whim of the architect's employer; and then a symmetrical front regular, to the utter inconvenience of the internal arrangements, is dressed up with tracery, battlements, and pinnacles; and these sit as uneasy on the modern block, as the chimney stacks and attics on an Albert Terrace Parthenon.

are so besotted in their mongrel compositions, that they tremble at the ascendancy of truth.[2]

The object of this tract is, therefore, to place Christian architecture

---

[2] It is a perfect disgrace to the Royal Academy, that its Professor of Architecture should be permitted to poison the minds of the students of that establishment by propagating his erroneous opinions of Christian architecture. The influence which his position naturally gives him over their minds is doubtless considerable, and the effect of his instructions proportionably pernicious. Not content, however, with the disparagement of ancient excellence, which he introduces in his official lectures, he is *practically* carrying out his contempt of pointed design in both Universities, and in a manner that must cause anguish of soul to any man of Catholic mind and feeling.

The ancient buildings of King's College, models of perfection in their way, are actually being demolished, to make room for a monstrous erection of mongrel Italian, a heavy, vulgar, unsightly mass, which already obscures from some points the lateral elevation of King's Chapel, and which it is impossible to pass without a depression of spirits and feelings of disgust. A man who paganizes in *the Universities* deserves no quarter; and it becomes a question whether the greater share of blame attaching to such transactions is due to the architect who could so wed himself to the bastard compositions generated in his studio, as to intrude his huge deformity not only in the vicinity but on the site of ancient excellence; or to the authorities of the University, who, in the very teeth of the present revival, have sanctioned so gross a violation of propriety. But their madness is paralleled at Oxford, where the same architect is erecting another unsightly pile of pagan details, stuck together to make up a show, for the university galleries immediately facing the venerable front of St. John's, and utterly destroying this beautiful entrance to the most Catholic-looking city in England. The pagan character of this edifice has, however, awakened the disgust of some of the most learned members of the University; and if it pleases the admirers of gin-palace design, it will draw down the indignation of every true disciple of Catholic and consistent architecture.

But, although some men, by dint of name, fortune, and station, may rule for a brief space, and mock that excellence to which they can never attain, yet their day is fast drawing to a close;—several of the junta who have disfigured the face of the country are already gone; and, like Bunyan's giants in the Pilgrim's Progress, the others are so enfeebled that they can only snarl at the revival of excellence. Their works will hardly be endured for the time they have to run, and the remembrance of them will be the laughing-stock of posterity; and when the ancient glories of our native land are restored, and this generation of pretenders have passed away, men will be amazed that a period could have existed when they were permitted to disfigure and destroy, unchecked and unreproved.

in its true position,—to exhibit the claims it possesses on our veneration and obedience, as the only correct expression of the faith, wants, and climate of our country; and if it fails in doing this, it will be rather owing to the incapacity of the author in doing justice to this most important subject, than to any want of truth in the proposition itself.

The arguments used, both by the advocates and opponents of pointed architecture, have been most fallacious. They have consisted, for the most part, in mere private views and opinions relative to comparative abstract beauty in the different styles; and these, as might be expected, have proved most inconclusive.

To advocate Christian architecture merely on the score of its beauty, can never prevail with those, who profess to think that all art and majesty is concentrated in a Grecian temple. We must turn to the principles from which all styles have originated. The history of architecture is the history of the world: as we inspect the edifices of antiquity, its nations, its dynasties, its religions, are all brought before us. The belief and manners of all people are embodied in the edifices they raised; it was impossible for any of them to have built consistently otherwise than they did: each was the inventor and perfector of their peculiar style; each style was the type of their Religion, customs, and climate. The abstract beauty of these various styles, when viewed with reference to the purposes for which they were raised, is great indeed; they are the perfection of what was intended: a follower of Bramah or Isis, a fire-worshipper of Persia, could not have produced any thing different from what they have done; and so truly did these edifices embody the principles and worship of their builders, that the discovery of a certain form of temple or peculiar symbols is at once admitted as evidence, of the existence of a certain people and religion in that place. Nay, more, by architecture and ornament alone, learned men of the present time are enabled to make the most important discoveries, relative to the history of nations, whose very existence is anterior by many centuries to the Christian era.

Will the architecture of our times, even supposing it solid enough to last, hand down to posterity any certain clue or guide to the system under which it was erected? Surely not; it is not the expression of existing opinions and circumstances, but a confused jumble of styles and symbols borrowed from all nations and periods.

Are not the adapters of pagan architecture violating every principle, that regulated the men whose works they profess to imitate? These uncompromising advocates of classic styles would be utterly repudiated by the humblest architect of pagan antiquity, were he now to return to earth. Vitruvius would spew if he beheld the works of those who glory in calling him master.

The restorers of Christian architecture are more consistent followers of classic *principles* than all these boasted Greeks; they understand antiquity, and apply the ancient consistent rules to the new dispensation. The moderns, in their pretended imitation of the classic system, are constantly producing the greatest anomalies; and we are called upon to admire their thrice-cooked hashes of pagan fragments (in which the ingredients are amalgamated in utter confusion) as fine national monuments of the present age.

I have not unfrequently been denominated by the perpetrators of these absurdities as a fanatic for pointed design, a blind bigot insensible to, and ignorant of, any beauty but that of the middle ages. So far from this, I much question, if I am not better acquainted with the principles on which the various styles of pagan antiquity were founded, than many of their warmest advocates. I believe them to be the *perfect expressions of imperfect systems*; the summit of human skill, expended on human inventions: but I claim for Christian art a merit and perfection, which it was impossible to attain even in the Mosaic dispensation, much less in the errors of polytheism. The former was but a type of the great blessings we enjoy,—the latter, the very antipodes to truth, and the worship of demons.

I can readily understand how the pyramid, the obelisk, the temple, and pagoda have arisen; whence the arrangement of their plan, and the symbols which decorate them have been generated. I am prepared to join in admiration at the skill which piled such gigantic masses on each other, which fashioned so exquisitely each limb and countenance; but I cannot acknowledge them to be appropriate types for the architecture of a Christian country.

If we worshipped Jupiter, or were votaries of Juggernaut, we should raise a temple, or erect a pagoda. If we believed in Mahomet, we should mount the crescent, and raise a mosque. If we burnt our dead, and offered animals to gods, we should use cinerary urns, and carve sacrificial friezes of bulls and goats. If we denied Christ, we should reject his Cross. For all these would be natural consequences: but, in the name of common sense, whilst we profess the creed of Christians, whilst we glory in being Englishmen, let us have an architecture, the arrangement and details of which will alike remind us of our faith and our country,—an architecture whose beauties we may claim as our own, whose symbols have originated in our religion and our customs. Such an architecture is to be found in the works of our great ancestors, whose noble conceptions and mighty works were originated and perfected under a faith and system, for the most part common with our own; for, strange as it may appear, the difference between us and our English forefathers, on examination, will prove slight indeed, compared with those nations, from whom we have been accustomed for the last century to borrow our types, as being the best suited to our present habits.

Before entering into the necessary details in support of this position, it may not be amiss to say a few words on the subject of Christian architecture. It has been frequently objected by the advocates of paganism, that the pointed style, especially Christian, was not developed till several centuries after the crucifixion of our Lord; but this is measuring the ways of God by mere human capacity. How long were the chosen people of God allowed to exist before the erection of the great temple of Jerusalem was permitted? Did not the skins of the desert typify the polished stones of that wondrous structure? And may we not say that the foundations of Cologne were commenced in the catacombs of the eternal city? Like protestants who rail at ecclesiastical solemnity, because it is not to be found in the persecuted church of the apostles, they urge the non-existence of spires under Roman emperors as a proof, that they were not generated by the Christian principle. But modern men are constantly referring to the church in her suffering state, described by our Lord under the similitude of a grain of mustard-seed, while they refuse to recognise her, when, as the greatest of all trees, she extended triumphant in beauty and luxuriant foliage over the earth.

How could the divine character of Christ's church have been made manifest to future generations, except by passing through an ordeal of poverty and bitter persecution of more than three centuries, and triumphing over the powers of the world and darkness, without human aid! Those were not, indeed, times for the cultivation of material arts; but the foundations of every Christian temple, spire, and pinnacle, were then laid so firmly, that we may build on them till doomsday without fear of sinking or decay. Byzantine, Lombard, Saxon, and Norman, were all various developements of Christian architecture on a cruciform plan with Christian symbols. Pointed architecture was the crowning result of these earlier efforts, which may be considered as the centering on which the great arch was turned.

The change which took place in the sixteenth century was not a matter of mere taste, but a change of soul; it was a great contention between Christian and pagan ideas, in which the latter triumphed, and for the first time *inconsistency* in architectural design was developed. Previous to that period, architecture had always been a correct type of the various systems, in which it was employed; but, from the moment the Christians adopted this fatal mistake, of reviving classic design, the principles of architecture have been plunged into miserable confusion. The gradual developement of inconsistent design is exceedingly curious.

At first it was confined to the substitution of a bastard sort of Italian detail to the ancient masses. This is particularly striking in the French buildings erected during the reign of Francis the First, where the high-pitched roofs, lofty turrets and chimney stacks, cresting buttresses, string courses, mullions, and all the natural and consistent features of ancient design, are retained with pagan capitals, friezes, and arabesques.[4] The church of St. Eustache, at Paris, is a most remarkable example of this period. It is perfectly Christian in its plan and arrangement, being cruciform, with double aisles and lateral chapels, a grand apsis and lady chapel, triforium, clerestory, pinnacles, flying buttresses, immense height, and all the features of a noble pointed church; but with debased Roman mouldings, cornices, and details, the very canopies over the images being composed of small pediments and domes. Thus, although the builders of the so-called *renaissance* opened the flood-gates of innovation, they had not lost *natural composition*; they only decorated what they required in an inconsistent manner: but the temple and regularity system had not come in. Indeed, we shall find that, down to the last century, many of the old principles were retained in both domestic and ecclesiastical buildings;[5] and it is only within a comparatively short time that error and inconsistency has attained its climax, by flattening and concealing roofs, disguising chimney stacks, building sham windows, compoing over brick walls, and dressing up Italian masses with pointed details, gathered from all styles, dates, and buildings.

[4] See Plate II.

[5] In several of the manor-houses erected during the seventeenth century, the chimney stacks are not concealed but ornamented, while the high roofs, gable ends, bay windows, turrets, and consistent features of the old domestic architecture, are all retained.

Wadham College, and the chapel of Brazennose, at Oxford, and the chapel of Peterhouse, Cambridge, may also be cited as illustrations of this fact.

Even in some of the older squares in London, such as Red Lion and Queen's, the houses had high roofs, with bold overhanging cornices and good dormer windows. Near New Street, Fetter Lane, some houses of this character are yet remaining, and are infinitely superior to the street erections of the present time.

CHRISTIAN ARCHITECTURE.

Never, in the annals of architecture, have so many glorious opportunities offered, in a short space of time, for the accomplishment of noble buildings. Within my own recollection, three royal palaces, half the metropolis, churches without number, vast restorations, entire colleges in both universities, galleries, civic buildings, bridges, hospitals, houses, public monuments, in every possible variety; and, with the exception of the New Houses of Parliament, we have not one edifice of the whole number that it is not painful to contemplate as a monument of national art. Every chance has been fairly thrown away, as it offered; of money, there has been an ample supply; for the cost of the various works has been something *enormous*; in all cases sufficient to have produced a good thing, and in many instances far more than was required. Now the cause of all these failures is the same, and may be summed up in three words, *inconsistency of design*. In no one instance has the purpose or destination of the building formed the ground-work of the composition: Grecian or Gothic, Ecclesiastical or Civil, it has been a mere system of *adaptation*. One man has adapted a temple, another a castle, a third an abbey; but temples, castles, and abbeys owed their existence to other wants and systems, foreign to those for which they have been employed, and utter failure is the natural result. Had the various buildings been allowed to tell their own tale, to appear in their natural garb, were it rich or simple, what variety and interest would our architectural monuments present!—but no, public buildings, it was said, could not be Gothic, and therefore must be Grecian, that is, with pediments and porticos. The reasons assigned were,—1st, That Gothic was so very expensive, which is a positive falsehood; and, 2ndly, That they would not be in character. Now, how an edifice that is to consist of doors, windows, walls, roofs, and chimneys, when consistently treated, and these various features made parts of the design, can be *less in character*, than a building where they are bunglingly concealed and disguised, it is impossible to imagine. Yet this view, so utterly false and absurd, has taken such hold on the minds of the million, that pointed architecture is considered, even at the present time, as out of the question when public offices, law courts, bridges, and similar structures, are in question; and the erection of the Parliament Houses in the national style is by far the greatest advance that has yet been gained in the right direction.[c] Although it is impossible to notice in the limits of this tract a hundredth part of the monstrous inconsistencies which are to be found in every modern erection; yet, to illustrate the truth of the position I have advanced, it will be necessary to notice some of the edifices that have been recently executed.

The Railways, had they been naturally treated, afforded a fine scope for grand massive architecture. Little more was required than buttresses, weathering, and segmental arches, resistance to *lateral* and *perpendicular pressure*.[f] I do not hesitate to say, that, by merely following out the work that was required to its natural conclusion, building exactly what was wanted in the simplest and most substantial manner,—mere construction, as the old men weathered the flanking walls of their defences, —tens of thousands of pounds could have been saved on every line, and grand and durable masses of building been produced; but from

---

[c] The long lines of fronts and excessive repetition are certainly not in accordance with the ancient spirit of civil architecture, but the detail is most consoling. We have the arms and badges of a long succession of our kings; images of ecclesiastical, military, and royal personages; appropriate legends in beautiful text run on every scroll: each emblem is characteristic of our country. The internal decoration is to be of a purely national character,—the absurdities of mythology utterly rejected,—and, if the architect's design for the great tower be carried out, we shall have a monument of English art which has not been surpassed even in antiquity. This building is the morning star of the great revival of national architecture and art: it is a complete and practical refutation of those men who venture to assert that pointed architecture is not suitable for public edifices; for the plan embodies every possible convenience of access, light, and distribution of the various halls and chambers, without the aid of false doors, blank windows, mock pediments, adapted temple fronts, and show domes, to make up an elevation.

[f] See Plate III.

inconsistency, whenever anything sublime has been attempted at the stations, the result is perfectly ridiculous.

In every instance the architects have evidently considered it an opportunity for *showing off what they could do*, instead of *carrying out what was required*. Hence the colossal Grecian portico or gateway, 100 feet high, for the cabs to drive through, and set down a few feet further, at the 14-inch brick wall and sash-window booking-office.[*] This piece of Brobdingnagian absurdity must have cost the company a sum which would have built a first-rate station, replete with convenience, and which would have been really grand from its simplicity. The Great Western stations, where any architectural display has been attempted, are mere caricatures of pointed design,—mock castellated work, huge tracery, shields without bearings, ugly mouldings, no-meaning projections, and all sorts of unaccountable breaks, to make up a design at once costly, and offensive, and full of pretension. Then the reasons which have instigated the various styles are so very absurd. At Rugby, because Rugby School, as rebuilt lately, has bad battlements and turrets, the old station had four half-turrets with the best side turned out, and a few sham loop-holes; a little further on, Gothic is dispensed with, and the barrack style prevails; at either end, two modern Greek buildings of colossal dimensions, both of which are utterly useless. The London gateway could not shelter a porter; while the Birmingham entrance was so unsuitable for its purpose, that the company have been obliged to erect various sheds right up to the large columns, and tack on a brick house, to make it at all available for its intended purpose.

These two gigantic piles of unmeaning masonry, raised at an enormous cost, are a striking proof of the utter disregard paid by architects to the *purposes* of the building, they are called upon to design; and many thousands have been fairly thrown away on every line in the erection of show fronts, and inconsistent and useless decoration.

[*] See Plate III.

The new Cemetery Companies have perpetrated the grossest absurdities in the buildings they have erected. Of course there are a superabundance of inverted torches, cinerary urns, and pagan emblems, tastefully disposed by the side of neat gravel walks, among cypress trees and weeping willows.

The central chapel is generally built on such a comprehensive plan as to be adapted (in the modern sense) for each sect and denomination in turn, as they may require its temporary use; but the entrance gateway is usually selected for the grand display of the company's enterprise and taste, as being well calculated from its position to induce persons to patronize the undertaking by the purchase of shares or graves. This is generally Egyptian, probably from some associations between the word catacombs, which occurs in the prospectus of the company, and the discoveries of Belzoni on the banks of the Nile; and nearly opposite the Green Man and Dog public-house, in the centre of a dead wall (which serves as a cheap medium of advertisement for blacking and shaving-strop manufacturers), a cement caricature of the entrance to an Egyptian temple, 2½ inches to the foot, is erected, with convenient lodges for the policeman and his wife, and a neat pair of cast iron hieroglyphical gates, which would puzzle the most learned to decipher; while, to prevent any mistake, some such words as "New Economical Compressed Grave Cemetery Company" are inscribed in *Grecian* capitals along the frieze, interspersed with hawk-headed divinities, and surmounted by a huge representation of the winged Osiris bearing a gas lamp.[y]

The new building of St. Paul's School is another flagrant instance of the inconsistency of modern design. No sooner had the architect received the commission of erecting a building for this ancient foundation, than he turned to his stale collection of pagan authors for the authorities and details of an edifice, that was instituted by one of the

---

[y] See Plate IV.

most pious churchmen of England for the education of Christian youths; and nothing better suggested itself to his narrow mind, than an unmeaning portico raised on stilts, serving only to darken the apartments over which it projects, an incipient dome, and a pagan frieze; and this wretched jumble of incongruities has cost twice the amount, and I speak advisedly, for which a truly appropriate structure, in accordance with the founder's intentions, could have been erected. It is probable that the architect never turned to study the life and intentions of Dean Colet, the learned and worthy ecclesiastic to whose pious munificence the school owes its existence, or he might have been moved to give some natural expression to the building which was intended to fulfil so pious a design. The intentions of the Dean were most edifying; the ancient edifice was dedicated in honour of the Child Jesus; the founder was evidently desirous of placing before the youthful inmates our Redeemer as an obedient Child, knowing all things, Lord of all, yet subject to his earthly parents. What could have been better calculated to have infused the principles of a holy life into the minds of the scholars? What edifying sculptures of the various incidents of our Redeemer's infancy might have ornamented the front of this building! Within the ancient school-room was an image of our Lord in the temple, teaching the doctors, before which the poor scholars sung a daily hymn and litany: but of all this not a vestige remains; and in lieu of holy Name or deed, we have fifty bulls' heads decorated for pagan sacrifice, *copied from the temple of the Sibyls*, with not so much as an image of the pious founder in a niche, to awaken the remembrance of departed worth in the hearts and minds of those, who daily benefit by Colet's bounty.

The new buildings of Christ's Hospital, although they certainly are free from the absurdities of paganism, are utterly deficient in the spirit of ancient design and arrangement. The opening towards Newgate Street might be mistaken for the back way to the Compter, or a place where relatives might hold intercourse with the inmates of that prison.

Although the tops of the posts which hold the gas lamps are ornamented with some canopy work, they look exceedingly modern, and are another striking proof of the inutility of employing the decoration without the spirit of the old men. The hospital being destined for a place of study and education, it should have been bounded towards the street with a lofty and massive enclosure wall, entered through a regular tower gate-house, like those in the Universities, with an image of the founder in a niche, the arms of the city and of the hospital in the spandrils, and appropriate legends and inscriptions.

One fine cloistered quadrangle of the original monastery was standing; another could have been added, with the refectory and necessary buildings, in the same severe style. The new dining-hall is designed on the very opposite principles to those which influenced the ancient builders. The walls of the old refectories *were comparatively low*, with a *high pitch of roof:* here, the walls are enormously high, with lofty windows, like a chapel, and covered by a flat roof; and, to make the case still worse, the roof of the building is not the ceiling of the hall, but this is a mere lath-and-plaster imitation, several feet below the actual covering.

This edifice is, moreover, only *Gothic on one side;* for, if by chance the spectator turns the corner, he perceives an elevation not at all dissimilar to that of the Fleet Prison towards Farringdon Street.[10] As for

---

[10] This wretched principle of making *pointed masks* for buildings pervades nearly all the designs of what are termed the leading architects of the day. They work only for show and effect, and neglect every portion of the building that does not meet the public eye. On going over Lambeth Palace, I was particularly struck, on opening a door from the new buildings (which are intended to be pointed, and externally have much good detail), to find myself in a kitchen court that might have been in the rear of the Euston Hotel. The architect had evidently laid aside his Gothic *domino*, and appeared in the regular sash-window style, while under the lee of his principal elevation; taking care, however, to resume his disguise as soon as he shot out into public observation. Now, although it would be most absurd and inconsistent to employ the same detail and enrichments on all sides of a building placed in an enclosed position, yet the spirit of construction should

the new dormitories and the buildings erected on the site of the old grammar school, they are strange piles of *debased* design; but in this respect the architect may have been influenced with reference to the period when the school was founded.

Altogether, the works of Christ's Hospital are sad failures, owing to their not being conceived in the ancient spirit; but still it must be owned, in justice, that when they were commenced, so little were the real principles of Christian architecture understood or recognised,[11] that

---

remain unchanged, even in the meanest offices. By simple chamfers and weatherings the mere essentials of good masonry, the character is perfectly maintained in every portion of the old buildings; and, what is most important, *naturally maintained*; that is, it would be impossible to do them better in any other way. *Details of this kind* do not require *designing*, but only *constructing*. For instance, the best gate must be the *strongest framed*; the sharp edges must be taken off the stiles and rails without weakening the joints and shoulders; they are chamfered and stinted, and the gate must and will look admirably well, and, of course, be in character with a pointed building, because a pointed building is a *natural building*. *In matters of ordinary use, a man must go out of his way to make a bad thing;* hence, in some of the rural districts, where workmen had not been poisoned by modern ideas; barns, sheds, &c., were built and framed, till very lately, on the true old principles, with braces, knees, and the high pitch. So little, however, have most modern architects any idea of beautiful effects that are produced by natural combinations and construction, that in most pointed buildings they design the mere fronts, and give up all these minor details in despair, as being so *expensive to carry out;* when, in fact, *treated consistently,* they *cost less* than the *ordinary sort of fittings, and are twice as durable*. This point is so important, that I trust, before long, to produce a treatise on *Natural Architecture,* where all those matters will be considered in detail.

[11] The progress which the revival of pointed architecture has made within the last few years is most surprising; and, if it goes on in the same ratio, there is no doubt that many architects of the day will hardly bear to look upon their present works in the course of a few years. In my own case I can truly state, that in buildings which I erected but a short time since, I can perceive numerous defects and errors, which I should not now commit; and, but a few years ago, I perpetrated abominations. Indeed, till I discovered those laws of pointed design, which I set forth in my 'True Principles,' I had no fixed rules to work upon, and frequently fell into error and extravagance. I designed and drew from a sort of intuitive feeling for Christian architecture, in consequence

it would have been difficult to have found any one, who could have done much better than the architect employed. It is a positive duty to point out all these defects, to prevent others from falling into similar errors; but, at the same time, we cannot but feel a personal respect for a man, who endeavoured to revive the old thing, at a time when there were few to sympathise or encourage.

The street elevations of the Bank of England are certainly the most costly masses of absurdities that have ever been erected. It appears to have been the aim of the architect to perpetrate as many unreal features as possible in a wall. Sometimes we have a row of *blank windows*; sometimes a *blocked-up entrance*, five feet from the ground;—now the wall is set back to diminish the internal space, and a row of columns occupies its place, well railed up to prevent any body getting under the recess;—now it rises up, to make a break, and support some stone urns and amphoræ, to hide the chimney stacks and skylights. But the grand feature is the N. W. angle, terminated by a portico, which, in addition to having *its doorway blocked up from the beginning, has its pavement several feet above the street*, without steps or means of access, *actually laid with spikes (!!!)* thickly interspersed with fragments of decaying orange-peel, stones, sticks, and bats, thrown there by the little boys, who used occasionally to climb up and get behind the columns before the introduction of the chevaux-de-frise.

It is impossible to state the vast sums that have been expended on the various absurdities of this inconsistent building; but, at a moderate

---

of the numerous examples I had seen. I entered into all the beauties of the style, *but I did not apply them with the feelings and on the principles of the old architects*. I was *only an adapter*, and often guilty of gross inconsistency. But, from the moment I understood that the beauty of architectural design depended on its being the expression of what the building required, and that for Christians that expression could only be correctly given by the medium of pointed architecture, all difficulties vanished; and I feel quite satisfied that when this principle becomes generally understood, good, consistent, and picturesque masses of building will arise, with all the variety and beauty of olden times.

computation, they would have erected the edifice, with all possible convenience and strength, and in a massive and appropriate character, three times over; and there then would have been, to use a commercial phrase, a good balance in hand for other purposes.

Unfortunately for themselves and the public, the Bank Directors appear to have more money than architectural judgment: hence, unmeaning features and details are crowded together, to make their buildings costly, and the Soanean eccentricities in which they have indulged so long seem only to have led them to continue the meretricious system under another management, if we may judge by the decorations of the New Dividend Office, where a room for the mere transaction of ordinary business is overloaded with all sorts of unmeaning plaster ornament, stuck up without the slightest propriety, or reference to the purpose of the building.

The Halls of the various Companies, that have been rebuilt at such an enormous cost, are really distressing to look upon. The origin and history of these companies, connected as they are with that of the City itself and many illustrious characters, afforded a fine scope for appropriate decoration, both in windows and on walls. For a hall, a noble roof of oak, with quaint device and legend, with Dais and Oriel, would seemingly have suggested itself as a matter of course to the architect, especially as many of the ancient buildings formerly belonging to these companies are actually figured in topographical works. The old kitchen, with its chimney and louvre, the buttery, and capacious cellarage in vaulted crypt beneath the hall, formed so many beautiful features of the ancient design; the rich sideboards of plate, the portraits of departed worthies, the banners and devices that hung aloft, the appropriate 'subtilties' that garnished the feast, are all described by the old chroniclers; the very barges still used by the companies might have suggested good ideas; but no,—a square mass, with a few meagre lines and breaks, Ionic caps and a flat pediment, is the extent to which the imaginations of the *great* architects of the day could reach; and at the main entrance into the city, one of the richest companies has erected a building vastly resembling the sort of edifices they set up for commercial banks in the larger provincial towns.

The present roof of the Guildhall itself is an abomination, and disgraceful to the civic authorities. The lower portions of the vast room are beautiful in character; and if the ancient roof was restored with all its appropriate devices, and enriched with colour and gilding, the Guildhall would be worthy of the city, and second only to the Regal hall at Westminster. The expense of its restoration would be a small matter to such a body, and the effect would surely far more than repay the outlay.

In the New Royal Exchange we have another stale dish of ill-adapted classicisms,—heavy, dull, and uninteresting,—nothing to awaken national or civic associations in the minds of the citizens. Surely the annals of one of the most ancient capitals of Europe might have suggested appropriate ideas for its Exchange, where the London worthies of successive centuries, with their bearings and devices, might have filled each niche. The effigies of these men, many of whom rose from poverty and obscurity, by humble industry, to wealth and high distinction, would serve as incitements for the imitation of this and successive generations. Every edifice, erected by such a body as the citizens of London, should embody the dignity and character of the first commercial city in the world; it should bear the impress of its antiquity, its honour, and privileges. Why should civic splendour be confined to an annual water excursion, or a single procession? The banners, the badges, the devices of the various Companies, Crafts, and Guilds, that compose the freemen of London, are beautiful and appropriate ornaments that should be carved on cap and wall, as well as painted on banner and scutcheon. Those who regard these matters as childish toys are surely mistaken in their estimate; they are honourable distinctions of skill and trade, invented by older and wiser men than most of those who compose this generation of innovators. They form the ties of fraternal intercourse and charity; they afford protection in decay and distress; and no one can have attentively perused the annals of London, and not admit that the various companies have been productive of immense good, and were mainly instrumental in preserving that honourable character which was formerly synonymous with an English merchant. The abuses that may at present exist among these companies, the degeneracy that is manifested in their buildings and ornaments, form no argument for their abolition. On the contrary, it should incite those in authority to revive the original practices and dignity of their various societies, and to invest their buildings, by appropriate decorations and symbols, with that local character and interest which was the distinguishing feature of the ancient buildings of London.

The absence of every thing in the architecture of the New Exchange calculated to awaken these local associations is truly lamentable. We see nothing but huge pilasters, cornices, columns, and pediments,—the same things that have been done one hundred times over, larger or smaller, in front of hotels, preaching-houses, news-rooms, and museums. It was a fine opportunity to have restored the arched ambulatory, buttressed quadrangle, high-crested roofs, and turrets of old English architecture, with a lofty clocher or bell tower, of grand proportions, like those which yet remain in the Flemish towns, and were formerly to be found in all our cities. This might have contained a fine peal to herald in the civic solemnities, with chimes for the successive hours of the day,—large clock faces, visible from all the cardinal points, and surmounted with a grove of gilded vanes, overtopped by the famous grasshopper of Gresham. Such a building, carried out with arms, badges, images, and appropriate detail, would have been at once an ornament and illustration of the city in which it was erected, admirably adapted for the convenience of business, and certainly not more, if so costly as the present unmeaning pile.

The faults of this, in common with modern structures in general, are not so much owing to individuals as to a system. How is it possible for any good results to be achieved with the present principles of architectural education? Can we ever hope to see a Christian architect come forth from the Royal Academy itself, where deadly errors are instilled into the mind of the student, with the very rudiments of instruction? Pagan lectures, pagan designs, pagan casts and models, pagan medals, and, as a reward for proficiency in these matters, a pagan journey! When the mind of a youth is well infused with contempt for every association connected with his religion and country, he is sent forth to measure temples, and, in due time, he returns to form the nucleus of a fresh set of small Doric men, and to infest the country with classical adaptations in Roman cement.

Of a truth, if architectural offices were stopped up, and fused as they serve wasp's nests in the country, we should be freed from a mass of poisonous matter that is still depositing in these places. God grant me the means, and I would soon place architectural studies on such a footing that the glory of these latter days should be even greater than that of the former.

I would also have travelling students, but I would circumscribe their limits. Durham the destination of some,—Lincolnshire's steepled fens for others,—Northampton spires and Yorkshire's venerable piles, Suffolk and Norfolk's coasts, Oxford, Devonshire, and Warwick, each county should be indeed a school,—for each *is* a school,—where those who run may read, and where volumes of ancient art lie open for all inquirers.[12]

Then would they learn that the same perfection of design is to be found in the simplicity of the village steeple, as in the towering central spire,—in the rubble walls of a sea-coast chancel, as in the hewn ashlar and fair mouldings of the large churches,—that consistency of architectural proportion has stunted the pillars of the simple nave, and

---

[12] When the architectural student was well grounded in the traditions of his national architecture, he should then proceed to study the grand continental cathedrals and churches, especially the flower and queen of Christian Churches, the Minster at Cologne.

roofed it with massive beams, while it has lifted the shafts of the cathedral to a prodigious height, and vaulted the vast space with stone,—that architectural skill consists in embodying and expressing the structure required, and not in disguising it by borrowed features. The peasant's hut, the yeoman's cottage, the farmer's house, the baronial hall, may be each perfect in its kind: the student should visit village and town, hamlet and city; he should be a minute observer of the animal and vegetable creation, of the grand effects of nature. The rocky coast, the fertile valley, the extended plain, the wooded hills, the river's bank, are all grand points to work upon; and so well did the ancient builders adapt their edifices to localities, that they seemed as if they formed a portion of nature itself, grappling and growing from the sites in which they are placed.

The rubble stones and flinty beach furnish stores as rich for the natural architect, as the limestone quarry or granite rock. What beautiful diversity does the face of this dear island present,—what a school for study and contemplation,—where are to be found twenty-four cathedrals, the finest monastic buildings, thousands of parochial churches, and interesting remains of antiquity without number, all within a boundary of a few hundred miles!

The student of Christian architecture should also imbue his mind with the mysteries of his Faith, the history of the Church, the lives of those glorious Saints and Martyrs that it has produced in all ages, especially those who, by birth or mission, are connected with the remains of ancient piety in this land. He should also be well acquainted with the annals of his country,—its constitutions, laws, privileges, and dignities,—the liturgy and rubrics of the Church,—customs and ceremonies,—topographical antiquities, local peculiarities, and natural resources. The face of the country would be then no longer disfigured by incongruous and eccentric erections, compounds of all styles and countries; but we should have structures whose arrangement and detail would be in accordance with our Faith, customs, and natural traditions. Climate would again regulate forms of covering, and positions of buildings. Local interest would be restored, and English architecture assume a distinct and dignified position in the history of art; *for we do not wish to produce mere servile imitators of former excellence of any kind, but men imbued with the consistent spirit of the ancient architects, who would work on their principles, and carry them out as the old men would have done, had they been placed in similar circumstances, and with similar wants to ourselves.*

The great objection raised against the revival of our ancient architecture by the advocates of paganism is the great difference between the present habits and necessities, and those which existed at the period when pointed architecture was most flourishing. But, in reply to this difficulty, to which I have previously alluded, it will not be difficult to prove, that while we have nothing in common with Pompeian villas and Greek temples, the ancient churches and mansions furnish us with perfect types for our present purposes; and, in order to illustrate this most important subject, I have set forth in detail the intimate connexion that can be traced between the existing system and English antiquity.

Ecclesiastical Architecture.

With that portion of the English clergy who have the happiness of being in communion with the Holy See, there cannot arise any doubt whatever. They hold precisely the same faith, and in essentials retain the same ritual, as the ancient English Church. They, consequently, require precisely the same arrangement of church, the same symbols and ornaments, as were general in this country previous to the schism. The various religious communities are bound by the same rule to recite the same office, and have the same duties to perform as those who erected and used the many solemn buildings,—now, alas! in ruins,—which are scattered all over the land. These, at least, cannot plead novelties for their paganism; and in the English Catholic body, any departure from Catholic architecture is utterly inexcusable. It can only be accounted for from extreme ignorance, or extreme perverseness, both reasons equally disgraceful. The plea of poverty cannot be admitted; for it is well known that churches which are erected on Catholic traditions are less costly than pagan rooms: and in Ireland, where the externals of religion are positively shocking and painful to behold,[13] immense sums, subscribed by the zeal of the people, have been squandered

---

[13] There is no country in Europe where the externals of religion present so distressing an aspect as Ireland:—in the rural districts, the extreme of poverty, dirt, and neglect; while, in the large towns, a lavish display of the vilest trash about the altars, and burlesques of classic or pointed design for churches, most costly and most offensive. A bad copy of that wretched compound of pagan and protestant architecture, St. Pancras New Church, in London, has been erected at Ardagh, and dignified by the name of a Cathedral. The Irish journals are lavish in their praise of this and similar structures, and boast of them as honourable examples of national skill, as if there was any thing *national* in these importations of English and continental abortions. If the clergy and gentry of Ireland possessed one spark of real national feeling, they would revive and restore those solemn piles of buildings which formerly covered that island of saints, and which are associated with the holiest and most honourable recollections of her history. Many of these were indeed rude and simple; but, massive and solemn, they harmonized most perfectly with the wild and rocky localities in which they were erected. The real Irish ecclesiastical architecture might be revived at a considerably less cost than is now actually expended on the construction of monstrosities; and the ignorance and apathy of the clergy on this most important subject is truly deplorable. They seem wedded to bad, paltry, and modern ideas; and this, too, with a people who are, perhaps, of all Catholic nations existing, the most worthy of solemn churches, and who would enter fully into the spirit and use of the ancient buildings, if they had them,—men whose faith no temporal loss or suffering could subdue,—who rise before daybreak and traverse miles of country to assist at the divine Office, and who would hail with enthusiasm any return to the solemn rites of their forefathers. If religion in Ireland were only to resume its ancient solemnity in externals, it would be indeed a spectacle for angels; but, at present, such are the absurdities, indecencies, and vulgarities displayed in all matters connected with Divine worship, that, notwithstanding the edifying piety of the people, and the exemplary conduct of many of the clergy, it is impossible to assist at the celebration of religious rites without feeling acutely pained and distressed.

on architectural absurdities. Hitherto the revival of Catholic art has been rather the result of amazing zeal amongst a few noble and devout individuals, than the spontaneous act of the body; and so-called Catholic periodicals must cease to talk of splendid Grecian altars, and solemn consecrations, where some fiddler and his pupil delighted the audience with their strains, before they can occupy their proper and dignified position as the restorers of Catholic architecture and solemnity. It is most consoling, on the one hand, to know that good ideas are spreading; but humiliating to think that there should be room for the spread of ideas and opinions which should fill the heart of every British Catholic, and animate them as one man in the glorious and holy cause. And, alas! whilst a few great spirits devote their fortune and energies for the revival of departed solemnity, others of equal temporal means are content to look on with apathy, if not actually to oppose their labours. Some apparently reject tradition and authority, espouse the cause of paganism, and follow in the wake of protestant monstrosities, with the externals of a temple, and the interior of a conventicle; while the multitude neither know nor care any thing about the matter. Men of devout minds are scandalized with the foreign trumpery that is introduced on the most solemn occasions, and the noisy theatrical effects that are substituted for the solemn chants and hymns of the Church. These things are most distressing on the continent, although they are modified by the vastness of the churches and the remains of antiquity; but here, in England, where they are performed in buildings not dissimilar to assembly-rooms, they are intolerable, and must convey to the casual and uninstructed spectator the lowest idea of Catholic rites. It is painful to see these wretched practices puffed off in Catholic journals, and described much in the same strain as is used in the Theatrical Observer,—a list of performers,—criticisms on the execution of solos and quartets during that Holy Sacrifice which fills even the angels with awe and reverence. Since Christ himself hung abandoned and bleeding on the Cross of Calvary, never has so sad a spectacle been exhibited to the afflicted Christian as is presented in many modern Catholic chapels, where the adorable Victim is offered up by the Priests of God's Church, disguised in miserable dresses intended for the sacred vestments, surrounded by a scoffing auditory of protestant sight-seekers who have paid a few shillings a head to grin at mysteries which they do not understand, and to hear the performances of an infidel troop of mercenary musicians, hired to sing symbols of faith they disbelieve, and salutations to that Holy Sacrament they mock and deny.

With respect to the present Anglican Church the case is, of course, by no means so clear and positive. Still, if she acted on her present acknowledged doctrines and discipline, without even taking into consideration any probable change in her position, she must turn to Catholic antiquity for the types of her architecture and ornament.

This argument is based on *principles and formularies;* for abuses cannot be either advanced or received in support of any position. I am not taking into account the various grades of opinion and practice that are unhappily to be found among those who act in the capacity of Anglican clergymen. I deal only with canons and rubrics; and if these were properly and universally carried out, a vast move would be made in the right direction.

1. The ancient form and arrangement of the parochial churches, consisting of nave and chancel, should be preserved. The words respecting the latter are as follow: "The chancels shall remain as in *times past;*"—and although it is a notorious fact that they did not so remain, yet their desecration was chiefly owing to the mass of illiterate functionaries, who, on the deprivation of the Catholic ecclesiastics under Elizabeth, were intruded not only into parochial cures, but into the chairs of the ancient bishoprics. In truth, the so-called reformers of the reign of Edward the Sixth and Elizabeth, and even the compilers of the Common Prayer itself, were far more protestant than the formularies which were retained, and to which they subscribed rather with the hope of being thereby able to effect further mischief and ad-

vance puritanism, than to restore departed solemnity.[14] Under the Primate Laud, a surprising re-action took place, unfortunate and unsatisfactory in result, but an evident proof of the Catholic feeling which would have developed itself in the Anglican Church, had it not been for the pressure of the puritan faction. But to return, taking the words as they stand,—*The chancels shall remain as in times past;*—can there be any reasonable doubt as to the propriety of adhering strictly to the ancient models, of which so many truly beautiful examples remain for imitation?

2. A tower for bells is required; and this important feature of a church was never omitted in England even during the most debased period of ecclesiastical architecture. A tower naturally suggests a spire as its termination; and where is it possible to obtain a consistent type for church steeples, excepting from those glorious churches whose entire architecture and arrangements were generated by the peculiar wants of Christian rites? This must be evident to all on inspecting the wretched attempts at classic steeples, where pediments and porticos, pillars and cornices, are piled upon each other like children's card houses, to make up an elevation without any grand connecting lines or consistent arrangement,—mere forced, unnatural combinations, most offensive to the eye, as evident endeavours to make a *vertical effect* out of the features of *horizontal architecture*. The rage for these pedimented and telescopic steeples is nearly over; and the ancient spire-crowned towers, adapted to any scale, or degree of decoration, must be universally restored.

3. Galleries are contrary to the intentions of the Anglican Church. They are of comparatively modern origin, erected for the most part since the Revolution; and their introduction can only be accounted for by a similar degeneracy of spirit to that which has tolerated them in so many modern Catholic churches, where they are far more objectionable and inconsistent.

---

[14] See the Letters of the intruded Bishops to Foreign Protestants, in Strype's Annals.

A most laudable opposition has, however, been awakened both against the erection of galleries and the modern abomination of pews, which are equally intolerable; and we may fairly hope before long to see both utterly abolished. It is not, therefore, difficult to show that an ancient church nave, with its pillars, aisles, low open carved oak benches, and southern porch, is the proper model for present imitation.

4. There is no alteration whatever allowable for ancient usage in respect of the Fonts: they are required to stand in their original position, with covers, and secured by locks. These covers may be made as lofty and ornamental as circumstances will admit. Many of them were executed during the reigns of James, and Charles the First; and although, of course, debased in details, are designed in the mass on the ancient principles, with a multitude of pinnacles and lesser canopies: of these there are two fine specimens at Newcastle-on-Tyne, and another, probably by the same artist, in Durham cathedral.

5. Pulpits, if properly placed on one side of the church, are not only unobjectionable, but necessary. Numerous examples, both of wood and stone, are to be found in the ancient English churches; and the ambones of the basilicas are of primitive antiquity. Pulpits are only offensive when intruded into the centre of the church, obscuring the Altar, and turning the back of the preacher to the seat of the sacred Mysteries; they should not be too elaborate in design, nor over large in dimensions. With respect to reading pew, and clerk's desk, they are of modern introduction; a brass or wooden lectern and a litany stool are amply sufficient. These are quite in accordance with ancient practice: the Epistle, Gospel, and Lessons were originally intended to be heard by the people, for which reason they were read from the top of the rood lofts in cathedral churches, where the choir was divided off by a close screen. The deacon, sub-deacon, or lector, out of respect for the Altar, read turned sideways to the people, while all prayers were addressed towards the East.

6. In many cases the chancel screens yet remain perfect, with much

of their ancient painting, gilding, and imagery of Saints and Apostles. They were *never removed in any case by authority*, but only from private ignorance, or love of innovation; and, so far from being opposed to Anglican custom, they are mentioned as necessary in old episcopal visitations. A screen of Italian detail, but of the old form, was erected during the last century in the church of St. Peter, Cornhill, London.

In old St. Giles's Church, Bloomsbury, erected in the seventeenth century, the chancel was separated by a large screen in the figure of a beautiful gate, on which were carved three statues,—on one side, St. Paul with his sword,—on the other, St. Barnabas with his book,—and over them, St. Peter and keys, with winged cherubim. This screen, erected at the cost of Lady Dudley, was pulled down in 1640, and sold by the puritan faction.[15] The choir screen of Wadham College Chapel, Oxford, consecrated in 1613, is a very interesting existing specimen of the continuance of the old traditional separation in the seventeenth century.

7. It is very certain that the consecrated stone Altars were sacrilegiously demolished and horribly profaned by the protestant party, both in Edward the Sixth's reign, and afterwards in the second year of Elizabeth's, and that their chief aim thereby was to abolish the idea of a sacrificial oblation among the people. But it is equally certain that their revival was attempted under a better state of things in the reign of Charles the First; and surely those who grant the authorities of Edward's time the right of demolishing, cannot deny the same right of restoration to their successors at a subsequent period. There can be but little doubt that stone Altars, placed at the eastern end of the chancel, will be generally revived; these may have frontals of the canonical colours, suited to the festivals, and richly embroidered with appropriate devices; and these frontals should not by any means be covered during the time of communion, as the white linen cloth need not be much wider than the top of the altar, and should hang down

---

[15] Parton's History of St. Giles's.

at each end. The use of lighted tapers on the altar seems to be warranted by the words, that such ornaments shall be in use, as were in use in the second year of King Edward the Sixth.[15] The candlesticks, covers of the holy gospels, chalices, &c., should be made of precisely the same form and decoration as those anciently used.

8. The two chairs, placed on each side of the communion table, are of very modern introduction, *and most unseemly*, as having their backs to the East. There can be no reason whatever for the clergy, when sitting, not occupying the sedilia, especially in cathedral churches, where the canon for the celebration of the communion requires the officiating priest to be attended by a gospeller and epistler (Canon xxiv.).

9. No doubt whatever can exist at the present time respecting the propriety of decorating churches with sacred symbols and imagery; the lively representation of the life of our blessed Redeemer, and the works and martyrdoms of the saints, cannot fail to be productive of much edification and good.

The destruction of the ancient stained glass, resplendent with sacred imagery, was mostly perpetrated by avowed puritans; and even at the worst periods there were found some good souls, who had both heart and means to preserve many of these glorious works from destruction. There are few cathedrals in Europe to compare in this respect to that of York; and many of our parochial churches are yet rich in glass. Indeed, when we reflect that during the last century the Catholic chapter of Amiens cathedral removed much of the magnificent glass of the nave, and replaced it by white panes, to *improve the effect*, and that modern Catholic ecclesiastics in France and Belgium have not only taken out the stained glass, but the mullions and tracery also, *by way of lighting the church*, we can feel less surprise at the sad losses we have sustained in England.

[15] Some excellent remarks on these and other matters connected with the celebration of the Anglican Liturgy are contained in two sermons preached in St. James's Church, Enfield. London, 1842.

In an admirable article which appeared in the British Critic, the writer most justly observes, that circumstances have so changed during the last three centuries, that some of the most violent innovators, had they lived in our age of lax indifference, would have acted and written in a very different strain. This remark will apply equally respecting the use of images. There is no fear at the present time of sacred representations being regarded with superstitious reverence: there is far greater danger that, holy symbols and figures being replaced by pagan fables or bare walls, men will lose all remembrance of the glorious mysteries they represented. It must be admitted that, in opposition to true Catholic doctrine, some images were regarded by the ignorant with a superstitious veneration, and certain representations were tolerated in the churches, which were highly objectionable. There can be but little doubt that all these matters would have been reformed, without violence or occasion of scandal to weaker brethren, by the decrees of the Council of Trent; and nothing can be more absurd and unjust than persons continually raking up, at the present time, old extravagant indulgences and local practices, which have been condemned centuries ago by ecclesiastical decrees, and some hundreds of which are denounced separately in works printed by authority.

The use and intention of sacred images is to raise the heart of the spectator from the figure to the reality, and to instruct the faithful in the mysteries of religion by lively representation. The soundness of this principle is fully acknowledged by the general practice of the present time,—in the multitude of biblical illustrations prepared for the instruction of youth.

The Church only requires that honour and veneration for sacred symbols which their character naturally demands,[17] and which is essen-

---

[17] This is beautifully expressed in the following distich, inscribed over a crucifix at Antwerp:

Effigiem Christi dum transis pronus honora,
Sed non effigiem sed quem designat adora.

tially the same as that yet given in the Anglican Church to the holy Name of Jesus; and is paralleled in temporal matters by the external respect shown to the throne in the House of Peers, or the quarter-deck of a man-of-war. Sacred imagery is a noble field for the exercise of the highest powers of art; and painting and sculpture, when devoted to the service of the Church, are calculated to improve and elevate the religious feelings of a nation in a surprising degree.

Now to sum up. If, as I have shown, the Anglican Church requires bell towers, spires, naves, chancels, screens, fonts, altars, sacred symbols and ornaments, I will ask whether the types of these various features are to be found in the ancient pointed churches of England, or in the classic temples of antiquity? Surely no one can hesitate to admit at once that, in the former, we have perfect models for imitation; while, in the latter, we cannot find one corresponding arrangement or detail; and therefore, even in its present position, by its own existing canons and rubrics, the Anglican Church is bound, consistently, to work exclusively on the principles of Christian architecture, and to renounce all pagan adaptations whatsoever.

With regard to the collegiate establishments which have continued in uninterrupted succession from the time of their original foundation, and which are yet supported by the pious munificence of their founders, and profess to be governed by their ancient statutes, there cannot exist a doubt as to the propriety, if not the absolute duty, of their erecting such buildings as they may require, in the same style and spirit as those originally raised for the accommodation of their predecessors. I say *spirit* as well as *style*; for it is not merely sufficient to cut tracery and build buttresses and pinnacles, for that has been done at a vast cost and with miserable effect at King's and other colleges at Cambridge, but to preserve that scholastic gravity of character, that reverend and solemn appearance, that is found in the ancient erections. Any departure from Catholic antiquity in a college is unpardonable: the frequent daily services in the chapel, the assembly of the community in the refectory, the enclosure, the academical costume, the celibacy of the inmates, are so many relics of ancient discipline which demand a continuance of the original architecture; and in those instances where this has been neglected, not one can be pointed out which is not a miserable failure and a compound of anomalies. Are Queen's, Worcester, or the new quadrangle of Christ Church, to be compared for one instant with Merton, New College, or Magdalene? They rather resemble sick hospitals or barracks of the last century, than the abodes of piety and learning. Colonnades, pediments, and heathen gods, are but sorry substitutes for solemn cloisters, high turrets, and images of reverend founders and saintly patrons.

During the early part of the seventeenth century, under the influence of the Laudian school, some collegiate buildings were erected in a far more consistent spirit than the more recent examples. Among these, the chapel of Peter-house, at Cambridge, is remarkable: the detail is, of course, debased, but it is a very successful attempt for the period; the tracery windows are filled with stained glass; the east window, of five lights, containing the Crucifixion of our Lord, with many saints and angels in the tracery. The roof is waggon-headed, supported on corbels; the western bay forms an antechapel, being divided off by an oak screen; within this are double rows of oak stalls, with a large sanctuary.

This chapel must have been far richer in decoration when originally founded; as, in the report of the parliamentary writers in 1643, they say, "We went to Peter-house and pulled down two mighty angels "with wings, and divers other angels, with the four evangelists, and "Peter with his keys, on the chapel door, together with about one "hundred cherubim, and many superstitious letters in gold." This account will show the correct intentions which actuated the collegiate builders of even that period, and how completely paganism was excluded from their designs: it is, indeed, monstrous, now that the ancient detail is so much better understood, and the facilities of execution far greater, to see vile compounds of Italian details rising amid the glories of Catholic antiquity in both Oxford and Cambridge. It is some consolation, however, to know that neither of these edifices are intended for collegiate purposes, but as show galleries; and I question much if they will be allowed to remain even for that purpose, when the true principles of Catholic architecture are more generally disseminated among the members of the University.

Hospitals for the poor ought, undoubtedly, to be erected in a style at once simple and religious; the aged should be provided with cloisters for sheltered exercise,—a common hall and kitchen,—separate lodging chambers, and a chapel for daily devotion; religious emblems and memorials of their benefactors should constitute the only decorations, interspersed with pious scriptures and moral legends. Beautiful examples of these truly Christian institutions are to be found in the ancient hospitals of Stamford, Leicester, Northampton, and Coventry, or even in the later foundations of Whitgift at Croydon, and Abbott at Guildford.

I trust I have now set forth enough to prove that the religious edifices of England, if consistently designed, should be arranged on the same principles as the ancient buildings erected by our Catholic forefathers. They must, of course, fall far short of the glorious solemnity that can alone be attained in a truly Catholic position; but, as far as they go, they should have all in common with English antiquity, and not the slightest accordance with classic arrangement and detail.

Sepulchral Memorials.

These are so intimately connected with ecclesiastical architecture, that it seems necessary to enter upon some details on the subject before proceeding to other matters.

The principal reasons assigned by sculptors for resorting to classic costume in their monumental designs has been the unsightly form of modern habits, which would render the effigy of the deceased ludicrous in appearance, if represented with them.

This would be perfectly true if it were necessary, or even correct, to adopt the ordinary costume of domestic life in such cases; but it is scarcely possible to find any person sufficiently dignified in station to warrant an effigy, who does not hold some official situation, either ecclesiastical, civil, or military; the robes and insignia of which, if properly and severely represented, would produce effigies little inferior in solemn effect to the ancient ones.[18] To represent persons of the present century in the costume of the fourteenth, is little less inconsistent than to envelope them in the Roman toga. As I have before said, architecture and art should be a consistent expression of the period, and it will not be difficult to show, that, adhering strictly to these principles, we can in the present age revive the most solemn and Christian memorials of the dead.[19]

ECCLESIASTICAL PERSONS.

For the English clergy, there is not the slightest difficulty; those in communion with the Holy See using the same number and character of sacred vestments as of old.

Bishops.—Amice, albe, stole, tunic and dalmatic, maniple, with chasuble or cope, mitre and staff, buskins and sandals.

Priests.—Amice, albe, plain or apparelled, stole, maniple and chasuble, holding a chalice with the most Holy Sacrament.

---

[18] The ancient monumental effigies invariably represent the deceased persons in their robes of state. Kings, bishops, priests, nobles, knights and their ladies, are habited in a manner to express most fully their dignities and office, with a profusion of heraldic devices illustrative of their birth and descent.

[19] The present female costume is by no means ill-adapted for sepulchral brasses. In the annexed Plate three are engraved, which are accurately copied from those in use. The devout position of the hands contributes greatly to the solemn effect. (See Plate **V**.)

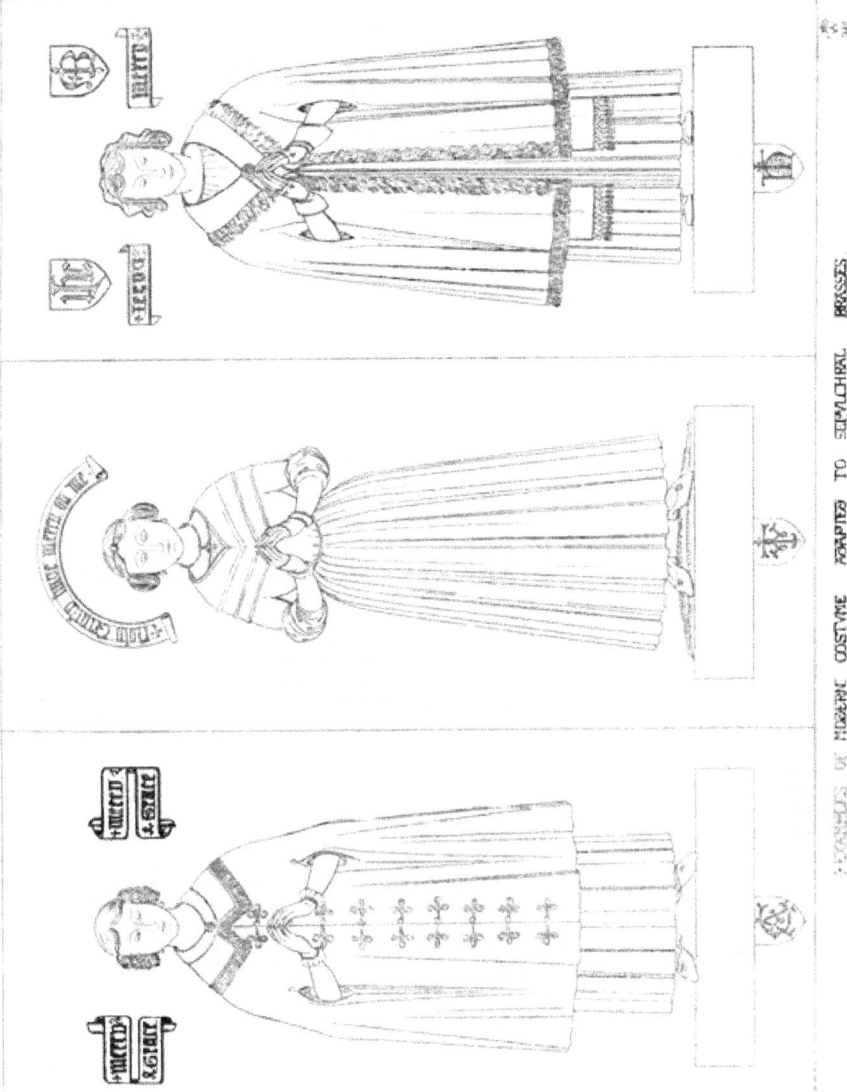

CHRISTIAN ARCHITECTURE.

Deacons.—Amice, albe, and dalmatic, stole and maniple, holding the book of the Holy Gospels.

Sub-deacons.—Amice, albe, tunic and maniple, with an empty chalice.

Minor orders. { Ostiarius, Lector, Exorcist, Acolyth } in surplices with { keys, book, hands joined in prayer, cruets and candlestick. }

These various dignities may be expressed, without effigy, by a cross fleury, with the pastoral staff, chalice, book, or other instruments represented by the side.

The Anglican churchmen should be habited as follows:

Bishops—in cassock, rochet, with a cope; and there are instances of the pastoral staff even in the seventeenth century.

Priests—in cassock, albe (plain), with a cope or chasuble.

Deacons—in an albe.

Effigies of clergy habited in surplices, with hoods,[20] would be perfectly correct, and of these there are many ancient examples.

These habits would be rather in accordance with Anglican *rubrics* than practice; but they are enjoined by the present canons, and, though long neglected, through the combined influence of indifference and puritan principles, they will be doubtless restored with the revival of reverence and solemnity.

CIVIL PERSONAGES.

The Sovereign should be represented in the Royal robes which are still used in the coronation, and which are precisely the same in number and description as those used in the days of St. Edward. There is no reason for not substituting appropriate and better designed ornaments in lieu of those which are generally embroidered, and a more beautiful form

---

[20] The present manner of wearing hoods hanging half down the back is most absurd. They should come close up to the neck, with the ends falling from each shoulder in front, as represented in the old monumental brasses.

of crown than that actually in use :[21] a recumbent effigy, habited in these robes, with the orb and sceptre, would not be inferior in dignity and effect to those truly royal monuments in Westminster Abbey Church, and would form an admirable contrast to the miserable memorials of the English sovereigns of the last century at Windsor.

The various ranks of nobility should be represented in the state robes peculiar to their several degrees, with their various family badges and heraldic distinctions; those who were Knights of the Garter or other orders, with their mantles, collars, and other insignia,—the lion and dog, emblems of courage and fidelity, couchant at their feet. When on high tombs, the niches round the sides may be most appropriately filled by smaller effigies of relations, habited as mourners for the deceased, with their several shields of arms. These are frequently introduced round the ancient monuments, and might be revived with the greatest propriety.

Judges should, of course, be represented in their robes,—Heralds, in their tabards,—Doctors of Medicine and Music, in the habit of their degrees,—Aldermen and civic functionaries, in their gowns of office;— and for private gentlemen even, a long cloak, disposed in severe folds, would produce a solemn effect.

For the humbler classes, a cross, with the instruments of their trades or crafts, with marks and devices, would be sufficient and appropriate; and, in a rural district, a mere wooden or stone cross, with the name of the deceased.

There is not, in fact, the least practical difficulty in reviving at the present time consistent and Christian monuments for all classes of persons,[22] and at the same cost now bestowed on pagan abominations,

---

[21] The present crown is far too heavy and clumsy, and is not very dissimilar in form to a lamp top. Still it is consoling to see that it is surmounted by a cross; and the circlet is yet alternated with crosses and fleurs-de-lis, emblematic of our Divine Redeemer and Blessed Lady.

[22] The annexed Plate represents brasses and other sepulchral monuments of a Christian character, that have been lately revived. (See Plate VI.)

+ REVIVED SEPULCHRAL BRASSES +

which disfigure both the consecrated enclosure which surrounds the church, and the interior of the sacred building itself. Surely the Cross must be the most appropriate emblem on the tombs of those who profess to believe in God crucified for the redemption of man; and it is almost incredible, that while the dead are interred in consecrated ground, and in the ancient position,—prayers for their souls' repose acknowledged to be of apostolical antiquity, and the office recited at their interment composed from the ancient ritual,—the types of all modern sepulchral monuments should be essentially pagan; and urns, broken pillars, extinguished lamps, inverted torches, and sarcophagi, should have been substituted for recumbent effigies, angels, and emblems of mercy and redemption.

Civil Architecture.

It will not be difficult to show that the wants and purposes of Civil Buildings now are almost identical with those of our English forefathers. In the first place, climate, which necessarily regulates the pitch of roofs, light, warmth, and internal arrangement, remains of course precisely the same as formerly. Secondly, we are governed by nearly the same laws and same system of political economy. The Sovereign, with the officers of state connected with the crown,—the Houses of Peers and Commons,—the judges of the various courts of law, and form of trial,—the titles and rank of the nobility,—the tenures by which their lands are held, and the privileges they enjoy,—the corporate bodies and civic functionaries,—are all essentially the same as in former days.

There is no country in Europe which has preserved so much of her ancient system as England. We still see the grey tower of the parochial church rising by the side of the manorial house; and, in many instances, the chantry chapel yet remains, with a long succession of family monuments, from the armed crusader to that of the parent of the actual possessor.

The palace of the Sovereign of such a country should exhibit the evidence of dignified antiquity in every detail. Surely the long succession of our kings,—their noble achievements,—the honourable badges and charges that they bore,—would form subjects which would naturally suggest themselves for the decorations of the various halls and apartments. How truly grand and national would a building thus designed and ornamented appear, where not only the general character, but every detail, was expressive of the dignity of the country, and an illustration of its history! And are not the examples for such an edifice to be found in the ancient glories of St. Stephen's and Windsor, the habitations of our Edwards and Henrys?—The mere dining-hall of the former, in its present denuded state, without tapestry, glass, or enrichment, conveys a far grander impression to the mind of the beholder than the most gorgeously decorated chambers of modern times; and what a splendid effect would be produced if one of those ancient palaces, so suited for the residence of a Christian monarch, were restored, with all its appropriate furniture and decorations!

The same remarks apply with equal force to the residences of the nobility and gentry. How painful is it to behold, in the centre of a fine old English park and vast domain, a square unsightly mass of bastard Italian, *without one expression of the faith, family, or country of the owner!* How contrary to the spirit of the ancient mansions, covered with ancestral badges and memorials, and harmonizing in beautiful irregularity with the face of nature!

Any modern invention which conduces to comfort, cleanliness, or durability, should be adopted by the consistent architect; *to copy a thing merely because it is old, is just as absurd as the imitations of the modern pagans.* Our domestic architecture should have a peculiar expression illustrative of our manners and habits: *as the castle merged into the baronial mansion, so it may be modified to suit actual necessities;* and the smaller detached houses which the present state of society has generated, should possess a peculiar character: they are only objectionable

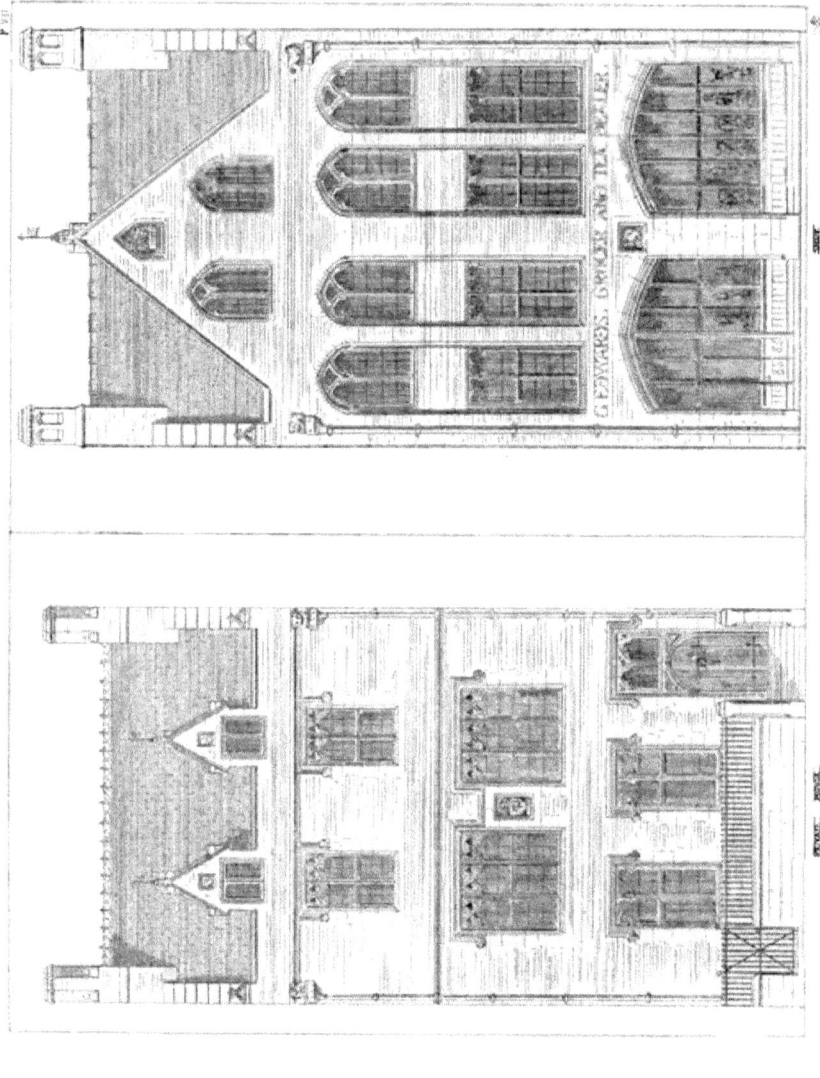

RECONSTRUCTED PRINCIPALS OF OLD DOMINICK ARCHITECTURAL ATELIER IN HIGHAM STREET EXETER.

when made to appear diminutive representations of larger structures. And it is not only possible, but easy, to work on the same consistent principles as our ancestors in the erection of all our domestic buildings.

It would be absurd, with our present resources, to build wooden houses in towns, which originated with the superabundance of that material in former times, and the difficulty of transporting stone or brick; but brick fronts, adapted perfectly to internal convenience, and in accordance with the legal provisions for town buildings, may be erected, which are capable of producing excellent effect, if consistently treated, and terminated by the natural form of the gable.[23]

There is no reason in the world why noble cities, combining all possible convenience of drainage, water-courses, and conveyance of gas,[24] may not be erected in the most consistent and yet Christian character. *Every building that is treated naturally, without disguise or concealment, cannot fail to look well.*

If our present domestic buildings were only designed in accordance with their actual purposes, they would appear equally picturesque with the old ones! Each edifice would tell its own tale, and, by diversity of character, contribute to the grand effect of the whole.

Modern Inventions and Mechanical Improvements.

In matters purely mechanical, the Christian architect should gladly avail himself of those improvements and increased facilities that are suggested from time to time. The steam engine is a most valuable power for sawing, raising, and cleansing stone, timber, and other materials. The old masons used wheels of great diameter in the erection of their buildings: this was, of course, a great increase of power over mere

---

[23] See Plate VII.

[24] A gas lamp, if designed simply with reference to its use, would be an inoffensive object; but when it is composed of a Roman altar, surmounted by the fasces, and terminated by an incense tripod, it becomes perfectly ridiculous.

manual strength; and had they been acquainted with a greater, they would undoubtedly have used it. Why should ten minutes be expended in raising a body which could be equally well done in two? The readier and cheaper the *mechanical* part of building can be rendered, the greater will be the effect for the funds; and if I were engaged in the erection of a vast church, I should certainly set up an engine that would saw blocks, turn detached shafts, and raise the various materials to the required heights. By saving and expedition in these matters, there would be more funds and a greater amount of manual labour to expend on enrichments and variety of detail.

The whole history of Pointed Architecture is a series of inventions: time was when the most beautiful productions of antiquity were novelties. *It is only when mechanical invention intrudes on the confines of art, and tends to subvert the principles which it should advance, that it becomes objectionable.* Putty pressing, plaster and iron casting for ornaments, wood burning, &c., are not to be rejected because such methods were unknown to our ancestors, *but on account of their being opposed in their very nature to the true principles of art and design,*—by substituting monotonous repetitions for beautiful variety, flatness of execution for bold relief, encouraging cheap and false magnificence, and reducing the varied principles of ornamental design, which should be in strict accordance with the various buildings and purposes in which it is used, to a mere ready-made manufacture. But while, on the one hand, we should utterly reject the use of castings as substitutes for ornamental sculpture, we should eagerly avail ourselves of the great improvements in the working of metals for constructive purposes.

Had the old builders possessed our means of obtaining and working iron, they would have availed themselves of it to a great extent. The want of proper ties has occasioned most serious settlements, and even the destruction of some of the finest Christian edifices,—the very weight and massiveness of the work causing it frequently to settle and give. And there is scarcely a tower of great dimensions erected during the middle ages, which it has not been necessary to tie together by iron chains and key wedges at a subsequent period. Now, it must be evident that if these ties were built in the first instance in the body of the work, they would be free from the action of atmosphere, and prevent both fissures and the spreading of the work which would render their ultimate employment necessary.

In a cruciform church these precautions are most necessary. The lateral thrust of nave, transept, and choir arches, both of aisles and triforium, rest against the four great central pillars, which are only enabled to resist the pressure by the weight of the great tower resting on them. But this in many cases was insufficient, and, when they began to give, has hastened their destruction. Hence the inverted arches at Wells, and the screens at Salisbury and Canterbury, which have been added long subsequently to the erection of the original buildings, to confine the pillars from giving inwards. At Amiens they are tied by immense chains extending the whole length of the nave and choir.

Had this point been considered in the original structures, the pressure might have been effectually counteracted, by inserting iron shafts in the centre of the great piers, and chains from them in the thickness of the triforium and clerestory, reaching to the four extremities of the building. I merely mention this one fact, amongst a number that might be adduced, to show that we possess facilities and materials unknown to our ancestors, and which would have greatly added to the stability of the structures they erected. *We do not want to arrest the course of inventions, but to confine these inventions to their legitimate uses, and to prevent their substitution for nobler arts.*

We approve highly of cast iron for constructive purposes, while we denounce it as the meagre substitute for masons' skill. We would gladly employ Roman cement in brick walling, while we abominate it in the mock erections of the day. We consider branding irons exceedingly useful for marking owners' and makers' names on carts and implements of trade, but we cannot allow them to replace the carver's art.

In a word, we should neither cling pertinaciously to ancient methods of building, solely on the score of antiquity, nor reject inventions because of their novelty, but try both by sound and consistent principles, and act accordingly.

Another great mistake of modern times is the supposition that Christian architecture will not afford sufficient scope for the art of sculpture. So far from this, while a Greek temple admits only of such decoration in the pediment and round the frieze, every portion of a Christian church may and should be covered with sculpture of the most varied kind,—vegetable, animal, and the human figure, in wonderful diversity of position and aspect; sometimes single in niches, sometimes in groups of high relief, and in subjects of the most majestic character. At the entrances of the church, the lessening arches, which form the vast recesses, are lined with angels, patriarchs, prophets, kings, martyrs, bishops, and confessors;[25] above the doorways, the genealogy of our Divine Redeemer, his birth, passion, the doom or final judgment,—subjects which, it must be admitted, afford the fullest scope for the developement of the highest powers of human skill. While the whole exterior of the sacred edifice, even to the summit of the towers, may be covered with images and sculpture, the interior presents an equally extensive field for the exercise of art in all possible variety of size and position, from the minute groups of the stall seats, to the long line of sacred history that surrounds the choir; from the enrichments of the aisle walls, level with the eye, to the sculptured bosses, luxuriant in foliage and rich in imagery, that key the vaulted roof at an immense elevation. Flaxman[26] was the first of

---

[25] Casts from some of these images at Notre Dame, Paris, which have lately been brought over to the School of Design, are wonderful examples of Christian art.

[26] Had Flaxman lived a few years later, he would have been a great Christian artist; but in his day men never thought it possible to do any thing fine in art that was not derived from paganism: hence his great powers were unhappily expended in illustrating fables of classic antiquity, instead of embodying edifying truths. His observations on the excellence of our Catholic ancestors, and his lamentations on the destruction of their works, are heartfelt

CHRISTIAN ARCHITECTURE.   43

the modern school who bore testimony both to the excellence of Christian sculpture and the scope that was afforded for the exercise of the art in pointed structures. His lectures contain several remarks on the admirable works executed in the English cathedrals, even while art was at a comparatively low ebb in Italy. There is in fact no difference of *principle* between the fine draperied works of the classic sculptors and those of the middle ages; the difference is in the *objects represented* and the motives of the artists. The principal object of the former was to display the human figure, which the latter, from the Christian principle of modesty, rather concealed. *The pagans wished to perpetuate human feelings,—the Christians, the divine.*[27]

But to talk of Gothic and Grecian drapery in sculpture as distinct in principle, is absurd; the art of either period *is a grand expression of nature*, and the distinct character is produced by the change of habits in the middle ages for those of classic antiquity. We have the cope instead of a toga, and the chasuble for a tunic. There is also a great difference in the texture of the various stuffs, the square folds of the Christian images being produced by the material then in use. Different circumstances and systems must generate different expressions of art. Phidias himself, had he worked under the influence of the Christian faith, would have exhibited equal skill in abstract art, but with a very different developement.

The great error of modern sculptors is their servile imitation of classic art, without endeavouring to embody existing principles in their works. Unless art is the expression of the system it should illustrate, it loses

---

and eloquent; and when we consider that at the period he wrote, the most glorious works of the middle ages were treated with apathy and even derision, the Christian artist of the present time must feel grateful for the good he effected by setting forth neglected truth. We can only regret that he did not follow out his convictions to their legitimate results, at least in the sepulchral monuments that were intrusted to him, for he does not appear to have executed one which had the slightest reference to Catholic traditions.

[27] See Plate VIII.

at once its greatest claim on admiration, and fails to awaken any feelings of sympathy in the heart of the spectator.

Since the fifteenth century, the saints of the Church have been made to resemble, as closely as possible, heathen divinities. *The Christian mysteries have been used as a mere vehicle for the revival of pagan forms and the exhibition of the artist's anatomical skill.* They were no longer productions to edify the faithful, but to advance the fame of the author; and all consistency and propriety was sacrificed for this unworthy end.[28]

The albe of purity and chaste girdle were exchanged for light and often indecent costume, to exhibit the human figure after the manner of an opera dancer; and modern artists were so imbued with classic design and ideas, that when they attempted to work for the Church, their representations of the mysteries of religion were scarcely recognisable from the fables of mythology.[29] We do not want to revive a facsimile of the works or style of any particular individual, or even period; *but it is the devotion, majesty, and repose of Christian art, for which we are contending:*—it is not a *style*, but a *principle.* Surely all the improvements that are consequent on the study of anatomy and the proportions of the human figure can be engrafted on ancient excellence; and an image, in correct costume, and treated in accordance with Catholic traditions, would afford equal scope for the display of the sculptor's art as a half-naked figure in a distorted attitude, more resembling a maniac who had hastily snatched a blanket for a covering than a canonized saint.

Did our artists of the present time work with the same faith and humility as the old men, and strive *to express the doctrines of the Church rather than their own peculiar notions,* we might soon have a school

---

[28] See Plate IX.

[29] It is but just to remark, that the modern German school, with the great Overbeck, are not only free from this reproach, but deserving of the warmest eulogiums and respect for their glorious revival of Christian art and traditions.

CONCEPTIONS OF ANGELIC SPIRITS BY OLD CHRISTIAN AND REVIVED PAGAN ARTISTS

of sculpture equal in sentiment and devotion, and superior in anatomical correctness, to that which existed during the ages of faith.

In conclusion, it must appear evident that the present revival of ancient architecture in this country is based on the soundest and most consistent principles. It is warranted by religion, government, climate, and the wants of society. It is a perfect expression of all we should hold sacred, honourable, and national, and connected with the holiest and dearest associations; nor is there in the whole world a country which is better calculated for the revival of ancient excellence and solemnity than England. We have immense power, vast wealth, and great though often misdirected zeal. Sounder views and opinions are daily gaining ground,—feelings of reverence for the past increasing in an extraordinary degree; and, with all her faults, we must remember that England, while she was the last to abandon Christian architecture, has been foremost in hailing and aiding its revival. Even in the worst and darkest times of pagan and protestant ascendancy, some of her sons were found able and willing advocates of her ancient glory; and, notwithstanding the repeated mutilations they have undergone, and the sad destruction of the monastic churches, our ecclesiastical edifices exhibit far more perfect traces of their ancient beauty than is to be found in many continental buildings, which, although they have escaped the hammer of the fanatic, have been more fatally injured from the chisels and pencils of revived pagan artists.

We should not try the deeds of England during the last three centuries by those which preceded them, *but by the corresponding history of surrounding nations;* and we shall find that throughout the Christian world, the period which has intervened since the sixteenth century has been one of bitter trial and degradation to the Church. Wherever we go, we see the great ecclesiastical works arrested at the same period,—towers half erected, naves unfinished, details uncarved,—either a total stoppage of works, or bastard pagan productions that had far better have been left undone. For a while throughout Europe, Catholic art and traditions lay neglected and despised, while paganism ruled triumphantly in the palace, penetrated the cloister, and even raised its detested head under the vaulted cathedrals and over the high altars of Christendom. When these lamentable facts are considered, together with the fearful scourge in the form of war and revolution that has passed over the countries of the continent, involving abbey and cathedral, church and convent, in one common ruin, and reducing the most dignified clergy of France to the condition of stipendiary clerks, sharing a miserable pittance with the Calvinist minister and Jewish rabbi, received from the hands of a government official,—not one rood of land left for priest or altar, of all the vast estates which ancient piety had bequeathed,—we may find cause for thankfulness that matters are not worse than they are in our own country.

The spirit of Dunstan, of Anselm, and St. Thomas, were extinct ere that of Cranmer could have prevailed. We must not forget that this country was separated from the Holy See by the consent of the canonically instituted clergy of this realm, with a few noble but rare exceptions. The people were actually betrayed by their own lawful pastors. There were no missionaries from the Holy See to dispense the sacraments to those who remained faithful. And this vital change was effected without the least external demonstration: protestant opinions were not even broached till some years after the schism; the externals of religion remained precisely the same; and even when open scenes of sacrilege and violence began, they were conducted in some measure by authority: mass was sung by the old clergy in Canterbury, while the bones of its saintly martyr were burning in the garth, and his name and festival were erased by the churchmen from every missal and breviary in the country; while men of family and distinction, professing the old faith, and receiving the sacraments according to the ancient ritual, shared the property of the Church with avidity. And if we may judge from the disgraceful trials that have lately arisen, many who bear the name of Catholic would rob the Church in her present need and poverty, as eagerly and with as little remorse as they did in the days of her former possessions. I mention these things, because it is a common error, into which I was formerly led, to cast the whole odium of the loss of the ancient faith in England on the king and nobles, whereas the Catholic hierarchy of this land, who basely surrendered the sacred charge they should have defended even to death, essentially contributed to the sad change. It is true they never contemplated the possibility of such a state of things as we see, or, indeed, which shortly succeeded to their base compliance; and many who had weakly consented afterwards rallied, but too late. It is a true saying, "*C'est le premier pas qui coute;*" and so indeed it turned out, to our bitter cost.

Regarding, therefore, the state of religion for the last three centuries as a punishment for the unfaithfulness of the English Church, we cannot but feel grateful that, notwithstanding all the repeated efforts and successes of the bitterest puritans, so many traces of the ancient paths have yet been preserved, to guide those who are now striving to regain the holy place. There is something surely providential in the retention of the ancient titles and dignities,—the daily chant of the divine office in the cathedrals and colleges,—the dedication of churches in honour of the ancient saints,—the consecration of ground for the burial of the dead,—the preservation of the chapel and order of England's patron, St. George,—the Catholic character of many portions of the liturgy, with its calendar of fasts and festivals,—the solemn service and anointing of the sovereign at the coronation. These, and many more, seem so many pledges that God will not be angry with this land for ever; for there is no other instance of a country having fallen into the miserable state of protestantism, having retained so much that is calculated to awaken in the breasts of her children a love and reverence for the past, and to lead them back to union with the see of blessed Peter, from whence the day-star of truth first beamed upon us.

Dugdale, Spelman, Bingham, Collier, Ashmole, and many illustrious English antiquaries and historians, might be cited to prove the great reverence for Catholic antiquity that was occasionally manifested in this country, even while the puritan faction was proceeding to violence. The spirit of Dugdale's text and plates is most Catholic; every line of his Monasticon might have been written in a cloister of ancient Benedictines, while his History of St. Paul's exhibits a depth of piety and devotion towards the glory of God's Church, worthy of more ancient days.

Spelman, in his works, expresses himself on the subject of sacrilegious spoliation in a manner that must strike shame and terror into the hearts of those Catholics who would spoil the Church of which they profess themselves the children; and he draws a fearful but true picture of the dismal disasters that befel the plunderers of the Church at the period of the general dissolution.

It is almost inconceivable that men, who had been educated in the principles of the ancient faith, who had partaken of the sacraments of the Church, and knelt at its altars, should have demolished, for the sake of stone, timber, and lead, edifices whose beauty and skill would have secured them from injury even in this generation, and which should have possessed in their eyes the highest claim on their veneration; and we can only account for the atrocities which accompanied the ascendancy of protestantism in England, by supposing the perpetrators blinded to the enormity of their own actions by the punishment of God. To hear of the choirs of vast churches stript and roofless,—tombs of prelates and nobles ransacked for lead,—brass rent from graves,—the consecrated vessels of the sanctuary profaned and melted,—the bones of saints and martyrs burnt,—the images of our Divine Redeemer trodden under foot, dragged about and consumed,—vestments converted to domestic use,—monastic libraries pillaged and burnt,—and all this without foreign foe or invasion, in once and then but lately Catholic England, and perpetrated by men who had been born and bred in the Catholic Church,—seems like a fearful dream, and almost incredible; and now the sad recital of destruction alone, moves us more than even the record of ancient glory: we lament over the prostrate pillars and scattered fragments of some once noble pile,—we raise the fallen cross,—bare the ancient legend on the wall,—collect the fragments from the shattered panes, and clear the accumulating soil from moulded base and tomb. The study of Catholic antiquity is so associated with ancient piety and holy recollections, that the soul is insensibly drawn from the contemplation of material objects to spiritual truths.

An Englishman needs not controversial writings to lead him to the faith of his fathers; it is written on the wall, on the window, on the pavement, by the highway. Let him but look on the tombs of those who occupy the most honourable position in the history of his country, —the devout, the noble, the valiant, and the wise,—and he will behold them with clasped hands invoking the saints of Holy Church, whilst the legend round the slabs begs the prayers of the passers-by for their souls' repose. At Canterbury he beholds the pallium, emblem of the jurisdiction conferred by St. Gregory on the blessed Austen, first primate of this land; at York, the keys of Peter, with triple crowns, are carved on buttress, parapet, and wall. Scarcely one village church or crumbling ruin that does not bear some badge of ancient faith and glory. Now the crosses on the walls tell of anointings with holy chrism and solemn dedication,—the sculptured font, of sacraments seven, and regeneration in the laver of grace: the legend on the bell inspires veneration for these consecrated heralds of the Church; the chalice and host over priestly tomb teaches of altar and sacrifice; the iron-clasped ambry, sculptured in the wall, bears record of holy Eucharist reserved for ghostly food,—the stoups in porch, and Galilee of hallowed water, and purification before prayer; while window, niche, spandril, and tower set forth, by pious effigies, that glorious company of angels, prophets, apostles, martyrs, and confessors, who, glorified in heaven, watch over and intercede for the faithful upon earth.

The Cross—that emblem of a Christian's hopes—still surmounts spire and gable; in flaming red it waves from the masts of our navy, over the towers of the sovereign's palace, and is blazoned on London's shield.

The order of St. George, our patron saint, founded by King Edward of famous memory, is yet the highest honour that can be conferred by sovereigns on the subject; and his chapel is glorious, and his feast kept solemnly. Our cities, towns, and localities, the rocky islands which surround our shores, are yet designated by the names of those saints of old through whose lives, martyrdoms, or benefactions, they have become famous.

The various seasons of the year are distinguished by the *masses* of these holy tides. Scarcely is there one noble house or family whose honourable bearings are not identical with those blazoned on ancient church or window, or chantry tomb, which are so many witnesses of the pious deeds and faith of their noble ancestry. Nay, more, our sovereign is solemnly crowned before the shrine of the saintly Edward, exhorted to follow in the footsteps of that pious king, and anointed with oil poured from the same spoon that was held by Canterbury's prelates eight centuries ago.

In short, Catholicism is so interwoven with every thing sacred, honourable, or glorious in England, that three centuries of puritanism, indifference, and infidelity, have not been able effectually to separate it. It clings to this land, and developes itself from time to time, as the better feelings of a naturally honourable man who had been betrayed into sin. What! an Englishman and a protestant! Oh, worse than parricide, to sever those holy ties that bind him to the past, to deprive himself of that sweet communion of soul with those holy men, now blessed spirits with God, who brought this island from pagan obscurity to the brightness of Christian light,—who covered its once dreary face with the noblest monuments of piety and skill,—who gave those lands which yet educate our youth, support the learned, and from whom we received all we have yet left that is glorious, even to our political government and privileges.

Can a man of soul look on the cross-crowned spire, and listen to the chime of distant bells, or stand beneath the lofty vault of cathedral

✠ CHVRCH FVRNITVRE REVIVED AT BIRMINGHAM 1848

choir, or gaze on long and lessening aisles, or kneel by ancient tomb, and yet *protest* against aught but that monstrous and unnatural system that has mutilated their beauty and marred their fair design? Surely not. And truly such feelings of reverence for long-despised excellence has been awakened among so many of our learned and devout countrymen, that we may begin to hope, indeed, that our redemption draws nigh. We have already lived to hear the name of Canterbury's blessed martyr pronounced with accents of veneration;—a hundred pens, most ably wielded, are writing in defence of ancient piety and practice;—a thousand voices are raised against the abominations of modern innovation. England is, indeed, awakening to a sense of her ancient dignity; she begins to appreciate the just merits of the past, and to work eagerly for the future. The last few years must, or ought to, have worked a great change in the feelings of English Catholics towards the Anglican churchmen; and it is evident that, if it be God's will that departed glories are to be restored, it will be effected rather by rebuilding the ruined walls of Zion than by demolishing the poor remains that are left. The tide of popular innovation that so lately threatened us with common destruction seems providentially stayed. God forbid we should endeavour to obtain a transept in a scramble with dissenters, but rather prove ourselves to possess the feelings of the true mother in Solomon's judgment, and freely give up all, than see what we hold so dear divided; and by perfecting ourselves, and carrying out true Catholic principles in charity, devotion, and zeal, hasten forward that union to which, in the words of an ecclesiastical periodical, we may even begin to look forward, and which is rather to be obtained through the sacrifice of the altar and midnight supplication, than by the clamours of an election platform or the tumult of popular commotion.

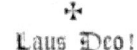

Laus Deo!

DESCRIPTION
OF THE
REVIVED CHURCH ORNAMENTS FIGURED IN PLATE X.

In the centre, a lectern of carved oak, surmounted by a cross fleury, with a double desk turning on the shaft. A Psalter and book of the Holy Gospels, bound with clasps, and bosses of gilt metal, enamelled and engraved, are shown lying on it.

Immediately over the lectern is a corona or circlet for lights, and on either side an altar lamp.

On the altar are various examples of altar candlesticks, and a small tower tabernacle for the reservation of the blessed Eucharist.

The frontal represents the four Evangelists and other sacred emblems embroidered in needle-work and gold. On the step, two high standing candlesticks for consecration tapers.

Curtains suspended to rods are shown on each side of the altar; and, immediately behind the candlesticks and tabernacle, a small reredos of gilt or embroidered work, over which is a ferettum or portable shrine.

On the right side of the altar—

 A processional cross.
 A pastoral staff.
 A faldistorium, with a precious mitre lying on it.
 A monstrance.
 Three chalices.
 A standing altar cross.

On the left side of the altar—

 A processional cross and a standing altar cross.
 A pastoral staff.
 A verge or cantor's staff.
 A ciborium.
 A pax and an Agnus Dei case.

On the pavement—

 Two thuribles, with a ship for incense, two holy water vats, a processional candlestick, a chrismatory, enamelled, and a sacrying bell.

These ornaments, and many others, have been most faithfully revived from ancient authorities by the care of a devout and skilful goldsmith of Birmingham, and are produced by the ancient methods of working metals.

www.ingramcontent.com/pod-product-compliance
Lightning Source LLC
Chambersburg PA
CBHW020230090426
42735CB00010B/1627